DATE DUE			

DIGITAL CAREER BUILDING™

CAREER BUILDING THROUGH

SKINNING AND MODDING

JERI FREEDMAN

ROSEN
PUBLISHING®

New York

Published in 2008 by The Rosen Publishing Group, Inc.
29 East 21st Street, New York, NY 10010

Library of Congress Cataloging-in-Publication Data

Freedman, Jeri.
Digital career building through skinning and modding /Jeri
Freedman.—1st ed.
    p. cm.—(Digital career building)
Includes bibliographical references and index.
ISBN-13: 978-1-4042-1354-8 (library binding)
1. Electronic games industry—Vocational guidance. 2. Computer
games—Programming—Vocational guidance. 3. Digital media—Vocational
guidance. 4. Web sites—Design—Vocational guidance. 5. Web site
development—Vocational guidance. I. Title.
HD9993.E452F74 2008
794.8023—dc22

                                                        2007027292

Manufactured in the China

CONTENTS

CHAPTER ONE

CHANGING THE DIGITAL WORLD

W hat do "skinning" and "modding" mean exactly? Which elements and skills involved in skinning and modding can be used in the career you choose?

Skinning

A "skin" is a set of elements you apply to an electronic device or to a set of Web pages. These elements are borders, colors, lettering styles, mouse cursor shapes, photographs, and other features. Skins allow users to change a Web page or program to suit their own tastes. Applying a skin is called "skinning." Skins are used to change the look and feel of desktop computers, media players, and instant-messaging applications.

(Above) The Mod DB Web site (www.moddb.com) provides a wide range of mods for some of the most popular games, including *Fallout* and *Half-Life*.

Media players are tools that allow users to play audio and/or video. Instant-messaging tools provide pop-up windows for conversing with your friends over the computer, just as you do on the phone. They act much like e-mail but work in real time, while both of you are connected. Some Web browsers (programs that allow you to surf the Internet) are skinnable, as are some Web sites, allowing a user to change the way the Web pages on the site appear on his or her computer.

Modding

In terms of software, modding is the process of creating a "modification" for an existing software program. In this context, it refers to a fan or user creating an add-on or module that can be used with a commercially available software program. Most "mods" are made for computer games. Mods range from very simple to highly complex. Some simply provide more weapons, equipment, or characters. Others consist of additional settings, dungeons, levels, and complete modules with their own storylines for existing games.

Many mods are distributed over the Internet. This may be done through a special location on the Web site of the company that manufactured the original game, or through an independent site created by fans of the original game.

History of Modding

Modding started in the 1980s. The practice began with hackers—individuals who use computers or computer code without permission. Hackers figured out how to

 Customize.org is an example of a site that provides online tools that allow you to alter images, such as a color-picker tool that lets you customize this wallpaper.

access source codes to popular games and change them. This meant that they could make modifications to the games' programming.

In the early 1990s, companies became more aware that players were interested in making their own variations. In response, some companies began selling their games with toolkits that allowed users to create their own modifications. Two of the earliest kits were the Bard's Tale Construction Set, by Interplay, and the dungeon construction kit for the *Forgotten Realms Advanced Dungeons and Dragons* computer games, by Strategic Simulations, Inc. The gamers' response was positive. It was easy to see that users had an avid interest in creating their own versions of a game's world.

TOOLS FOR SKINNING AND MODDING

Here's a selection of Web sites that provide skins and modding tools:

- Customize.org (www.customize.org): This site offers a list of new skinning products available from other sites, as well as downloadable icons, skins, and themes.
- FileFront (www.filefront.com): This site provides mods, maps, and skins and tools for creating them for popular games such as *World of Warcraft* and *Half-Life*.
- Gamespy (www.gamespy.com): This site provides subsites called Planets with mods and modding tools for games such as *Elder Scrolls Oblivion* and *Morrowind*.
- Megagames (www.megagames.com): This is a source for mods and modding tools for many popular games.
- Mod db (http://mods.moddb.com): This site provides tutorials in mod making, new mods, and mods to download.
- Mod the Sims 2 (www.modthesims2.com/wiki.php?title=MTS2: Create): This site provides mods and tools for modding *The Sims*.
- Real (http://realone.real.com%3Fsubsection+skins): The maker of the RealPlayer media player that runs on Windows offers the RealSkins Toolkit on its Web site, allowing you to customize your RealPlayer.
- Simmers Paintshop (www.simmerspaintshop.com): This site provides downloadable tools for creating skins for flight simulators.
- Stardock (www.stardock.com): This site provides a tool called ObjectDock that allows you to create a customized desktop on your computer.
- Winamp (www.winamp.com/skins/create.php): This site provides two online tutorials on how to create Winamp skins.
- *World of Warcraft* (http://wowui.incgamers.com): This site provides tools for modding *World of Warcraft*.

A gamer playing *The Sims 2*. *The Sims* series has inspired a huge number of mods, including new settings, possessions, and furnishings.

In the mid-1990s, another company, id Software, included modding software with its games. Two of id Software's most popular modifiable games, *Doom* and *Quake*, are still popular.

In 1999, the computer game *The Sims* spurred modding to new heights. This world of virtual people whose lives are controlled by the player naturally lends itself to add-ons. As soon as the game came out, players started creating mods that would add new props, settings, and other elements. In the 2000s, the vast interest in altering games led manufacturers to start publishing advanced toolkits along with their games. Among the most popular games that are modded are *Half-Life* (Valve Software), *Unreal Tournament* (Epic Games), *World of Warcraft* (Blizzard Entertainment), and *Elder Scrolls: Oblivion* (Bethesda Softworks).

How Modding Has Changed Computer Gaming

For many players, a game no longer ends when they solve the final quest or defeat the last unit of an army. Numerous games are sold with tools that help modders create their own versions of various game elements. In addition, fan sites exist for many popular games. Players can go to these sites to download mods and tools to create their own mods. They can exchange ideas with others who are interested in the same game. As a result, computer gaming no longer means plunking down $50 for a game you'll play only once. The basic game has become a gateway into your own fully customizable world.

Modding and the Computer Game Industry

When fans started making modifications for computer games, the game companies responded negatively. They saw modding as a threat to their copyrights. A copyright is a legal right that allows only the owner of the copyrighted material to reproduce it.

WATCH OUT The game you mod is the property of the manufacturer. You cannot sell the mods you make without the manufacturer's permission. Manufacturers may have other rules regarding how you can distribute mods, such as requiring users to own a copy of the game.

Some console game manufacturers, such as Sony (PlayStation 2), Nintendo (Wii), and Microsoft (Xbox), are still resistant to the idea of mods. They fear that if hackers get access to their codes, the result will be a flood of fake game cartridges.

Personal computer (PC) software manufacturers are another matter. Over time, many game companies have come to realize that allowing mods can be a valuable form of advertising. Modding gets more people involved in buying different versions of the main game, as well as expansions. However, computer game manufacturers also have to protect their property. Some have attempted to take control of the modding process by providing modding kits with the games. They may also provide game forums on their Web sites—places where fans can exchange information. In this way, modding can take place with the involvement of the company that produced the game.

This gamer is using a Nintendo Wii game console. Console manufacturers like Nintendo discourage modding in order to protect their technology.

Other companies are publishing games along with tools that aid users in making mods. Some are simple, like the "mapping" tools that allow users to create their own dungeons or settings. Others allow access to development tools that let users create complete add-on modules.

TECH TOOLS If you're interested in modding a game, check out the Web site of the game's manufacturer. Often, there is a link you can click on to request a software development kit (SDK). The SDK will provide you with the tools to mod the game. Some publishers require you to purchase a copy of the game to get the SDK.

Computer game companies that allow the distribution of mods require that they be available for free, not sold. For the game industry, this means that the life of a game continues even after the manufacturer has placed its product on store shelves.

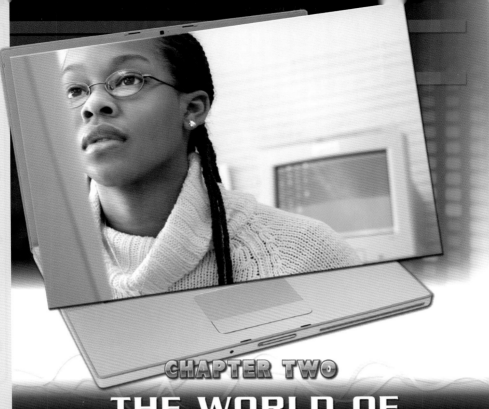

CHAPTER TWO

THE WORLD OF DIGITAL DEVELOPMENT

An interest in skinning and modding may lead you to a career in either Web site design or computer game development. This chapter explores these two fields and the types of jobs available in them.

Careers in Web Design

In a small company, one person may play multiple roles. But in a large company, or in a company that does Web site development for other businesses, a person may take only one of the professional positions that are described in this section on Web design.

Some who create Web sites for a company are salaried, in-house employees. Others are freelancers—

(Above) As Web sites, computer games, and computer animation become more advanced, there will be more and more careers opening in these fields.

workers who are self-employed and typically provide services to many different companies. Freelancers usually bill on an hourly basis for the time they spend working for a company. The drawbacks of freelancing are that you do not receive company-provided benefits, such as health insurance. In addition, you alone are responsible for advertising and marketing your services to get enough work to support you. The advantages of being a freelancer are that you are your own boss and can schedule your work as you wish.

Web and User Interaction Designers

In many ways, Web design is similar to customizing your own Web page or handheld electronic device, using skins. Web designers are in charge of the overall appearance of a company's Web sites. Most companies have a public Web site that customers can access to learn about the company and its products and services. It is also common for companies to have a private Web site, called an intranet. This is a network that only employees, and sometimes business partners or suppliers, can access. Internal sites may provide information on the company's activities that affect employees. Designers of these sites first observe how users work, then they create sites that are comfortable and easy to use.

What the Web designer does is similar to skinning. He or she applies themes, colors, logos, and decorative elements that give the pages on the Web site a look and feel that are appropriate for the company the site is created for.

 An important part of Web site design is working with users and managers to figure out what design will best meet their needs.

Web Developers and Programmers

People who create Web sites are called Web developers or Web programmers. Their job is to write the programming code to create the company's Web sites. They update the sites regularly, removing old information and adding new information. Web programmers may maintain the databases (stored data) accessed by users of a site.

Many careers in Web design have come to exist only in the past decade. Now, Web pages often include elements like animation, which have changed the skills required in the field. It is quite probable that as technology continues to change, new careers will appear.

Careers in Game Design

When you create mods, you use many of the same skills and tools that are used to design computer and video games. Planning a story, creating objects, animating characters, and painting scenery are all part of making both a mod and a game for sale. If you use a software toolkit provided by a game manufacturer to create your mod, you are even using some of the same tools.

Unlike creating a mod, however, making a full-blown game is not usually the work of one person. Today's computer games feature advanced graphics and real-time game play. For this reason, creating them requires more than one programmer sitting down at one computer. An entire team of professionals can be involved in creating a game. As a result, there are many different types of careers in computer gaming. The types of mods you like to make may give you some idea of what career would interest you.

The game industry is one of the fastest-growing segments of the entertainment industry. Many young people are excited by the idea of getting paid to work on computer games. For this reason, there is a lot of competition for entry-level jobs in this field. The better developed your skills are, the more you will have to offer a potential employer.

This section describes some of the diverse jobs that exist in the computer gaming field. Working on mods for current games is one way of keeping abreast of the latest products and leaders in the industry. This is key because being up-to-date on things is important when looking for a job.

People in the game industry are aware of what's happening in the modding scene. For example, in his "Homebrew" column for *PC Gamer* magazine, Brett Todd highlighted the modding work of twenty-one-year-old Cameron Sneed. Working with the game *S.T.A.L.K.E.R.: Shadow of Chernobyl,* Sneed developed a mod called Float32, which improves the look of the game's graphic images. Imagine what a help it is when looking for a job to have had your work featured in a national magazine!

QUICK TIP The online classified ad sites Craigslist (www.craigslist.org) and Monster (www.monster.com) contain hundreds of postings for computer industry jobs and are good places to look for job leads.

Game Designers

The game designer, logically, is responsible for developing the overall design of a game. This includes the concept, the type of content, and the way the game play will work. Game designers map out the concept of the game in writing. They are to games what the writer is to a movie. Game designers must be able to visualize what a game will look like. At the same time, they must be able to express their ideas in writing. If you write your own mods, you are developing skills in design. These include planning the sequence of events in your mod and creating new characters or settings. In this way, making mods can give you experience in planning a project, similar to designing a game.

Using modding tools on your own will have you working with many of the same digital tools used in graphic design classes like this one.

QUICK TIP Companies invest enormous sums of money in the development of a new game, so they can't afford to produce games that don't sell. They're more likely to hire you if you've already proved your ability in game development. Designing a game mod that becomes popular with other users is one way to do this.

Digital Artists

Producing imaginative settings and objects is one of the most creative areas of computer modding. If you are more interested in creating images than in the planning and programming aspects of making a mod, you may be interested in being a digital artist. Modding can give you experience in the following skills:

- Mapping—creating a digital layout, or map, with all the elements that will appear on the screen
- Modeling—forming objects of all types, including people
- Texturing—using color, light and shadow, and other visual effects to create surfaces
- Animation—making objects and characters move, for example, creating rippling water

There are tutorials online at sites such as Games Modding (www.gamesmodding.com). They offer instructions on using specific software and techniques to create visual effects.

A digital modeler works on a character in the *MySims* game being developed by Electronic Arts. If you like working with figures and color, digital art can be a creative and satisfying career choice.

Digital artists use the same types of software that modders use to create the detailed environments you see in a computer game. Images that are created digitally are called computer graphics. Digital artists use computer graphics software to create two-dimensional images and three-dimensional environments. In addition to computer gaming, digital artists can find careers in motion-picture animation. Their skills also are needed in the advertising industry and in public relations, a field in which people create a positive image of a person or product.

Game Developers/Programmers

Game programmers, sometimes referred to as game developers, do the actual work of creating the game. If you make mods for computer games that add new chapters to the story or new functions to the game, you are doing computer programming. In making your mods, you will use special digital tools provided by the game's manufacturer. Or you may learn programming languages, such as C++, that allow you to create mods from scratch. Game programmers use the same types of tools to create commercial games. With computer games becoming more complex, it is not unusual for programmers to specialize in a specific aspect of game programming. It is also common for numerous pro-grammers to work on different parts of a game at the same time. Some of the different aspects of game pro-gramming are:

• Animation—creating a sequence of graphics that, when run together, give the appearance of movement

VIRTUAL LIFE TO REAL WORK

Will Wright, creator of *The Sims*, with a screen from the game at Maxis Studios in Walnut Creek, California

Several leaders in the computer game industry started out by modding the games they played. In his teens, John Carmack managed to access the source code of games he played so he could give his characters new skills. He later became lead programmer on the landmark game *Doom*. Now, he tries to design the code in his games so that players can make mods without damaging the core game. In a *Popular Science* article, "The Mod Squad," Carmack told author David Kushner, "Putting these capabilities into the hands of users, the game becomes a new canvas for people."

Similarly, game creator Will Wright got into game development through a form of modding. Way back in 1984, he was playing *Raid on Bungeling Bay* on the Commodore 64, one of the earliest personal computers. Wright discovered that he preferred creating new levels for the game to actually playing the game. This eventually led him to design *SimCity*, a game that allowed users to create their own cities. He formed the company Maxis with investor Jeff Braun to publish the game. Wright later joined Electronic Arts and produced the mega hit *The Sims* in 2000. That project spawned numerous expansions and became one of the best-selling games of all time.

 A sound engineer adds sound to a computer game. Sound development is an area in which you can practice techniques used in the field when making mods.

- Sound—creating realistic and effective voices, noises, and sound effects
- Artificial intelligence—programming that allows a computer to make decisions
- Physics—programming that allows characters and objects in a game to behave in a lifelike manner
- Data input—using input from a variety of devices, such as a keyboard, joystick, or mouse.

Modding can give you the opportunity to try out all of these aspects of game programming. This provides you with valuable experience in different types

This gamer is playing *Counter-Strike*, one of the most successful mods of all time. Creating a mod like this requires all of the skills necessary to create a professional game.

of programming and tools. It also allows you to discover what type of programming interests you most.

Game Tester

Although game testing may seem like the most amusing aspect of game development, it's not. Game testing requires you to play parts of a game over and over as it's developed. As you go along, you record errors, known as "bugs," and provide that information to the programmers. The programmers then fix the bugs, and the game tester then retests that part of the game. This position requires tolerance for doing the same thing over and over for long periods. It also requires attention to detail to catch

HALF-LIFE TO WORK LIFE

Minh Le and Jess Cliffe are excellent examples of people who got started in their careers by writing a computer mod. While in college, they worked together on the now-famous Counter-Strike mod for the game *Half-Life*, produced by the Valve Corporation. Le became friendly with Cliffe, a Web programmer who maintained the Web site for *Action Quake 2*, a mod of the popular game *Quake II*. Together, Le and Cliffe created the Counter-Strike mod, releasing it in 1999. After graduating in 2000, Le landed a job with Valve. Cliffe, too, graduated from college and got a job at Valve.

all the potential problems—we all know how much we hate it when a bug shows up in a game. Game testers do not use all of the tools used by digital artists and designers. However, the best game testers are familiar with a variety of digital tools and applications. A tester who knows a program's capabilities will be better at suggesting fixes for bugs.

CHAPTER THREE

EXPOSURE

The Web and computer gaming fields are constantly changing. Staying involved with your chosen area through skinning and modding can give you an advantage over other potential employees. It allows you to demonstrate to a prospective employer that you understand what is currently being done in the field and that you are capable of working in it.

Building an Electronic Portfolio

A portfolio is a collection of work you have done. To create an electronic portfolio, you select your best creations and put copies of these files on a CD. This can be done using the built-in file-copying functions of Windows or

(Above) The Themes Gallery at www.belchfire.net. Many sites let users upload desktop themes, wallpaper, and screensavers so you can share your work.

Mac operating systems. When looking for a job, you can give a copy of the CD to potential employers to show the type of work you can do.

Your electronic portfolio may contain a complete mod that is like a new chapter in a game, or you might have a small mod that adds new characters, skills, or objects to a game. On the other hand, you may have created a map that provides a new area in which to play. Your portfolio may contain a screensaver or some other useful or interesting graphic using images from a game. If you are interested in a particular area, such as computer artwork, your portfolio can include a collection of different types of work to show that you have a broad range of skills.

Becoming Part of the Modding Community

Being an active member of the modding community can help you in two ways. First, most work in the computer field today is done by teams of people working closely together on various aspects of a project. So, cooperation on a project in a modding community can help you develop essential teamwork skills. In addition, it demonstrates to future employers that you have the ability to work well with others.

Second, being active in the modding community can be a valuable form of networking, or connecting up with other people with similar interests. People you get to know may go on to work in the field, where they could be valuable contacts when you are looking for employment. In addition, being part of the modding community for a popular game may give you the opportunity to

 Jordan Mechner, designer of the popular *Prince of Persia*, got his start through a game he designed while still a college student.

develop contacts at companies that have employees who communicate with modders.

Jordan Mechner, designer of the computer/console game *Prince of Persia*, provides an example of how doing work on your own can bring you to the attention of companies. As a teen, Mechner liked to make up computer games. When he was still in college, he created a game set in ancient Japan called *Karateka*, using the basic programming languages available at that time. He put a copy of the game on a floppy disk and sent it to the game company Broderbund. Broderbund was so impressed that it hired him for a summer job and published his game. Interestingly, Mechner got his college degree in psychology, not computer science. This supports the claim made by many professionals in the field that knowledge of history, philosophy, and psychology is necessary to make great games.

WATCH OUT Never copy a game and distribute it with a mod. Doing so is a violation of the manufacturer's copyright. Original work created by an individual or company is protected by copyright laws. If you use someone's work without permission, you may face legal penalties such as fines or even imprisonment. In addition, the company that holds the copyright can sue you in court, and you could be required to pay the company for misusing its property.

Online Exposure

The greatest joy in modding is sharing your work with others and receiving positive feedback. Most major games

A forum at www.gaspowered.com. Forums on modding sites can provide you with access to others who may be able to help you work out problems in the mod you're developing.

have sites where you can post skins and mods. Most sites also have forums, or pages where people can post comments and suggestions. While we all like admiration, placing your work on a Web site also lets others give you ideas on how to improve it. If it is thoughtful and constructive, feedback will help you develop your skills and become a better designer and programmer.

QUICK TIP Most experts in the computer game industry point to a high-quality demo as a key element in choosing candidates to interview for jobs. Use the knowledge you gain from feedback online to improve the quality of your work.

Helping others is important, too. In the software development community, the group that supports the development of free programs often develops a great respect for those who contribute. Games are no exception. If you do first-class work and contribute regularly, you can gain recognition for the quality of your work. A reputation as an asset to the gaming community can only help you when you are searching for a job.

Good Modding Etiquette

Etiquette means "proper behavior." Remember that the game you are modding is not your property. Even if a manufacturer makes a software development toolkit or Web site available to help you mod a game, it does not mean that anything goes. Show good etiquette by obeying the manufacturer's rules for creating and distributing mods.

Many video game manufacturers do not welcome modding of their games. Unlike computers, most video game consoles use proprietary (private) technology that is closely guarded by a corporation. Therefore, you need to get written permission before modding certain games. If you mod a video game against a company's wishes, you can be prosecuted for violating copyright.

The same applies to using material that is owned by other parties. You could run into trouble if you use licensed characters owned by companies other than the game manufacturer. For example, if you put *Star Wars* characters in your non–*Star Wars* game mod and distribute it, you could get into trouble with Lucasfilm. Be careful about using characters from TV shows, books, or movies that are not already part of the game.

SKINNING AND MODDING

Characters such as Yoda are property of the company that created the original movie, television show, or book. You must have permission to use such characters in your mods.

Finally, it is just good manners to respect the game company's work. Creating mods with nudity, vulgarity, or other offensive material is showing disrespect for a company that is trying to work with you. Why would you want to hurt a company when it is trying to provide you with games that you want to play? Why would you want to anger people who could help you establish a career?

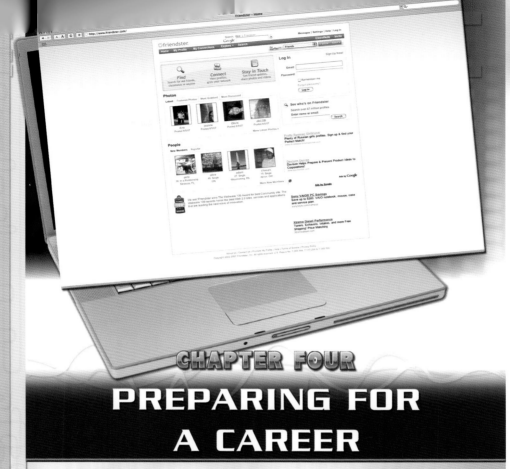

CHAPTER FOUR

PREPARING FOR A CAREER

You say you love to customize your digital world, and you want a career that will let you use your computer skills. This chapter discusses what you can do to get that dream job in the computer industry.

Programming Languages

To prepare for a professional position in any software-related field, you will need to learn at least a couple of programming languages. Among the most commonly used languages are C# and Visual Basic (for Windows computer systems) and Linux (for Unix systems). If you want to create Web pages, the common tools used for this purpose include hypertext markup language (HTML),

(Above) A Web page on Friendster.com. Professional Web pages are created with the same tools you use to create skins.

```
<p class=heading-2>How do you identify passive
sentences?</p>
<p class=body-text>Passive sentences have two basic
features, although both do not appear in every passive
sentence.</p>
<p class=body-text style="margin-left: 18pt;">1.</p>
<p class=body-text style="margin-left: 36pt; margin-top: -
12pt;">A past participle (generally with "ed" on the end);
and</p>
<p class=body-text style="margin-left: 18pt;">2.</p>
<p class=body-text style="margin-left: 36pt; margin-top: -
12pt;">A form of the verb "to be."</p>
<p class=body-text> In a very few instances, passive voice
may be appropriate. For example, when one action follows
another as a matter of law, and there is no actor (besides
the law itself) for the second action, a passive sentence
may be the best method of expression.</p>
```

A page of hypertext markup language (HTML) code used to create a Web page. HTML controls the way text is presented on the screen, allowing you to create a specific look.

extensible markup language (XML), and cascading style sheets (CSS). These are the same languages used to create the skins that you apply on Web pages. Clearly, customizing your own Web page with skins and making your own skins are great ways to gain experience in using these tools.

Programming languages can be learned at home using self-teaching books, some of which are written specifically for young people. *Web Design for Teens, 3D Game Programming for Teens*, and *Game Art for Teens* all provide a detailed introduction to using programming languages and other software creation tools. There are also Web sites that provide online tutorials. W3Schools, for example, has tutorials for learning XML (www. w3schools.com/xml) and HTML (www.w3schools.com/ html), as well as cascading style sheets (www.w3schools. com/css).

Junior High and High School

Unfortunately, technical knowledge of computer languages and tools is not enough to succeed in a career in the Web design or computer/video game fields. A broad range of knowledge is required. If you feel sure that you want such a career, it's never too early to begin preparing for it.

If your school offers a class in computer science, then this is a natural choice for you. However, your job in junior and senior high school is not to become a computer expert. Rather, it is to gain an education in basic skills that are critical to success. First and foremost, you need to learn good written and spoken communication skills, so you need a thorough understanding of English. You also need to learn how to organize your ideas and present them clearly.

QUICK TIP

If your high school offers a course in typing, take it. If you pursue a career in the computer field, you'll spend a lot of time at the keyboard.

If you plan to work in any hands-on aspect of Web page or game programming or development, you will need strong math and computation skills, so take all the math courses you can. If you are interested in pursuing a career in digital design or art, then take art courses,

SKINNING AND MODDING

Keyboarding (typing) is a skill you will use in all computer-based jobs. Take your computer assignments seriously, and practice this skill every chance you get.

either through your school or through outside programs. As you learn about the principles of good design, you can practice by making mods.

Learn as much as you can from the courses you take in history, social studies, and literature. If you want to create computer games, then the more you know about these topics, the better. Ideas and knowledge are power. Computer games, even the ones set in fantasy and future environments, often are based on historical situations in different cultures. For the same reason, studying literature and mythology is beneficial. If you make game mods, you'll rapidly see how important knowledge in areas like history is to developing content. After all, a game mod has to be about something.

After-school activities can be sources of learning that will be useful in developing computer games. Sports such as martial arts, fencing, and gymnastics may provide you with handy knowledge about the body and movement that you can use in a game.

After High School: Types of Schools and Programs

Many colleges offer bachelor's (four-year) degree programs in computer science for those interested in digital design and development. Technical institutes have four-year degree programs as well. Many also offer associate's degree programs, which are shorter college programs that concentrate on particular technical skills. Degree programs are available in areas such as digital 3-D design, digital graphic design, digital multimedia design, digital video animation design, Web design, multimedia (programs that combine audio, video, and/or text), Web development, game design, and game development.

INTERNSHIPS

A challenge you may face in getting your first job is competing against applicants who already have job experience. One way you can gain experience is through an internship at a company. As an intern, you will perform entry-level tasks in your chosen field and observe how things are really done in the industry. If you work hard, an internship can provide you with a good job reference when you're looking for your first "real" job.

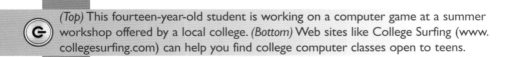

(Top) This fourteen-year-old student is working on a computer game at a summer workshop offered by a local college. *(Bottom)* Web sites like College Surfing (www.collegesurfing.com) can help you find college computer classes open to teens.

Visit the College Surfing Web site (www. collegesurfing.com/ce/search/design/?ip = 68.239.42.154&src = &) or the Web Design School Review site (www.webdesignschool review.com) to learn more about schools that offer digital design classes and degrees.

College for Web Design

If you plan on heading to college, you will want to take courses that provide you with specific knowledge that will be useful in your chosen career. College is an excellent place to learn how to do things thoroughly and on time, which will serve you well in the highly competitive computer field.

For Web design in particular, you will need to take programming courses in the languages used to create Web sites. As mentioned previously, some common languages include HTML, XML, and CSS. A course in visual composition will be helpful for understanding what makes for good visual design. This type of course should be available through the art department.

College for Computer Gaming

In addition to computer technology courses, many designers and artists in the computer gaming field take film production classes. This is because telling a story through a computer game is in some ways similar to telling a story through film or video. Visuals, sound, acting, and writing are all key aspects of telling a story in both types of media. Therefore, learning the elements that allow you to plan a film well can help you do the same in a game.

If you are interested in becoming a digital artist, you will need to take courses in computer graphics, 3-D modeling, and animation. You will probably want to take art courses in order to learn the skills necessary for effective visual design. These skills include the use of color and light, and the art of composition, or the way to arrange visual elements effectively. You may want to take courses in music and sound effects, since these elements are widely used in computer games.

Are you interested in the production side of computer games? Then you will need to take courses in the programming languages commonly used in the field, including C and C++. Many computer game companies are involved in developing games for multiplayer use. Therefore, a course in programming for computer networks can help make you desirable to future employers.

Remember that college is about learning, not just getting a job. If you apply yourself, you can demonstrate that in addition to specific knowledge, you can plan, execute, and follow through to achieve a goal. This makes a good impression on potential employers.

A Broad Background

Some of the most successful people in the computer field have studied a wide range of subjects, not just computer science or design. Steve Theodore, for example, is an animator and character designer for Valve Corporation. He has a bachelor's degree in classics and a master's degree in Roman history. Raphael Baptista, general manager

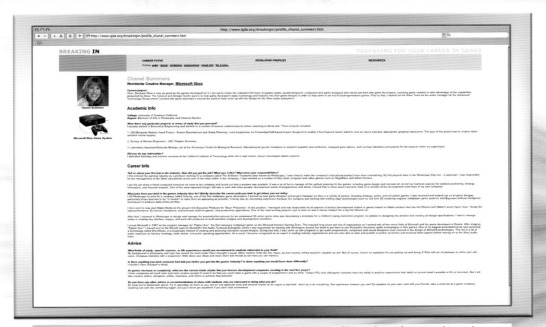

The IGDA Web site (www.IGDA.org) provides profiles of professionals with advice for students. The page shown here features Chanel Summers, worldwide creative manager for Microsoft Xbox.

and lead programmer of Helixe software, has a bachelor's degree in linguistics. Chanel Summers, worldwide creative manager for Microsoft Xbox, has a bachelor's degree in philosophy and classical studies. Seonaidh Davenport, program manager for Microsoft Games, has a bachelor's degree in the history of art and architecture.

A broad knowledge base is ideal for creating interesting and diverse games. Knowing some psychology can be useful for creating believable game characters. In Web design, too, knowledge of psychology can help you understand people and how they react to different types of visual and audio elements. This could enable you to create a successful user interface. In the field of computer and video gaming, knowledge of biology and physics often turns out to be valuable. Even subjects that may seem irrelevant can show you different ways of thinking that you can apply to your own field. This will allow you to make connections and solve problems in new and creative ways.

CHAPTER FIVE

WORKING IN THE DIGITAL WORLD

When it comes to looking for work, you can check the want ads in the newspaper. If you live near a major city, there may be companies advertising for Web designers. Game companies may or may not be located in the city where you live.

Finding a Job in Digital Development

In addition to looking in the newspaper, there are several other ways you can go about looking for a job in digital design and development:

- Your school may have a placement office that helps students find internships and jobs.

(Above) Online job sites like Monster.com are a major source of employees for companies in the computer and software industries.

Craigslist CEO Lim Buckmaster *(left)* and founder Craig Newmark *(right)* publish the world's biggest source of online classified ads.

- Online services such as Craigslist.org and Monster.com have become common places for companies to post job openings.

- Recruitment agencies (sometimes called head hunters) are often hired by larger companies to find employees. You can get a listing of recruitment agencies from the phone book or by doing a Yellow Pages search on Yahoo! or Google.

- Networking can be one of the most successful ways to find a job. If you have developed industry contacts while modding, put them to work for you! They can be a valuable source of job leads.

Presenting Your Work

Experts agree that having a portfolio of work to show potential employers is key to getting an interview that could lead to a job. If you do skinning and modding, then you have a great opportunity to create work that highlights your abilities. Along with a portfolio, you'll need a resume. This is a document that lists part-time or internship job experience and your educational background.

You can provide examples of your work in several different formats. For example, you can provide sample Web pages or digital artwork as a slide show, using a presentation program such as PowerPoint by Microsoft, or printouts of your online work. As mentioned earlier, you can provide a CD with digital art or a demo of computer game mods. Remember that quality is more important that quantity. The work you submit to a potential employer should be your best.

Working in Web Design

You probably are curious about what it's like to have a job that uses the skills you honed by skinning and modding. Let's start by looking at the position of Web designer. This person designs Web sites to meet the goals of the company. The process usually starts with meetings with senior management to establish the goals for the Web site and the type of image the company wants.

Are you mostly concerned with creating and applying skins to make your own Web pages? Or are you more interested in making and customizing Web pages for your friends? If you enjoy working with people as well as

 Web developer Justin Kitch (*above*) engineered a way to let clients build their own Web sites using designs by professional Web designers.

skinning or modding, you may want to pursue user interface design. As a user interface designer, you may meet face-to-face the people who will use the Web site you design. You observe how they perform the activities that the site will offer, and then you create an appropriate design for them. For example, if a company is creating a shopping Web site, you may observe the steps that people have to go through to locate, select, and pay for items. You may provide samples of computer screens to see what users and management like and dislike about the design.

A Web designer uses the software tools and languages described earlier, as well as programs such as Dreamweaver and Flash, by Adobe. These programs allow audiovisual elements to be placed into a Web site. The Web designer shows the proposed design to management and often goes through several rounds of review before that design is finalized. The Web designer then creates the skins that give the Web site its unique look and feel. These will be applied to all the Web pages that make up the Web site.

For a better idea of what Web design tools are like, take a tour of Dreamweaver by going to www.adobe.com/products/dreamweaver and clicking the "Take a Tour" link.

Web designers do not always do the actual programming required to make a Web site perform a specific task. That work is left to Web developers and programmers. A Web developer or programmer will spend a lot of time writing code to make the Web site function. This involves taking the design for the site and writing the actual code that will make it perform the functions required. If you enjoy the hands-on process of making Web pages for yourself and your friends, or making your own skins to apply to your Web pages, then you may be interested in Web programming.

Working on Computer Games: Game Designer

The game designer develops the overall concept of a game and describes it in writing. He or she creates written technical specifications, or "specs," for programming the game. He or she may create storyboards (illustrations of actual screens) showing some of the key features of the game. Often, the design of the game will be refined

A young programmer at work. Your first job will most likely have you performing basic programming or digital art tasks.

through a series of meetings with managers and others involved in the game's creation. Once management has approved the design, digital artists and programmers create the actual product. Game designers do not actually do the programming. But it is important for them to understand what is possible and desirable to include in a game from a technological point of view. Therefore, some knowledge of the programming tools used to create games is necessary.

Working on Computer Games: Digital Artist

Once the specs have been completed, it is up to digital artists to design and create the actual elements of the

The KatsBits Web site (www.katsbits.com) provides tutorials in creating digital 3-D models, a common task for digital arts in the computer game industry.

game. In the early days of computer gaming, a digital artist might have created the entire setting for a computer game. As the graphics used in games have become more complicated, this process has changed. Today, teams of artists create a setting. An individual may specialize in only one aspect of the creation—either modeling (creating the 3-D structure of elements in a setting), texturing (creating 3-D effects with characteristics such as shadows), or animation (movement). All of these skills are used in making mods. You might use software supplied by the manufacturer or another company to make a model of the objects in the setting. Then you might color them to give them a certain look. You

Experienced digital artists are responsible for modeling and texturing complex video images.

are developing 3-D modeling and texturing skills when you do this. Web sites like GamesModding.com provide tutorials on creating various visual effects, including adding dust motes or creating shadow effects. If you can do these things in your mods, you should be well prepared to learn how to use the more advanced tools to do the same thing on the job.

Working on Computer Games: Programmer

As with Web programming, game programmers write the actual code that produces the game world and characters and makes all the elements work as described in the design specs. Often, a programmer will write code that controls one specific aspect of the game. Such a standalone unit of code is referred to as a module. As programmers write code, game testers test the various modules and record any errors, or bugs, they find. The programmer then fixes the bugs and returns the module to the game tester for more testing. This process is repeated many times until the code works well.

Dream Job or Nightmare?

Working on computer games often requires long hours, especially as the deadline for the publication approaches. It commonly takes several years to design, develop, and test a game. Therefore, it is a long-term commitment on the part of the people working on the project. Working on a computer game can be interesting and creative. However, there is often a lot of pressure involved in working on such a project. Deadlines must be met, and since many companies in the field are small or medium-sized, meeting deadlines for a game's release can be

TYPES OF JOBS AND PAY RANGES

According to the "6th Annual Salary Survey" published by *Game Developer* magazine, the following are average pay ranges for jobs in the computer game industry. Salaries increase with the number of years of experience.

- Programmer: $58,000–$89,000
- Artist or animator: $45,000–$72,000
- Game designer: $46,000–$67,000

Those who become directors of departments typically earn $10,000 to $20,000 more.

According to The Information Architecture Institute's salary survey, in 2006, Web designers and developers with a bachelor's degree earned from $45,000 to $65,000, approximately, and those with a master's degree earned from $85,000 to $129,000, depending on their years of experience.

In addition to base salary, it's common for professionals in these fields to receive another $5,000–$10,000 in the form of:

- Bonuses— extra money paid for meeting particular goals
- Royalties—a small percentage of the money earned by a product
- Stock options—the right to purchase shares of the company's stock at a reduced price
- Profit sharing—a percentage of the profit that the company makes annually

critical to the companies' financial survival. Some hire employees on a long-term basis, just like any other business. In smaller companies, however, team members may be hired for the duration of a project and laid off once that project is over. Thus, staying in this field may mean limited job security and a lot of moving around from one company to another as projects begin and end.

QUICK TIP If you are working as a member of a production team, try to maintain a pleasant relationship with the people you work with and for. In the computer industry, people move around a lot, and you may meet former coworkers and managers when you are applying for a future job.

In your first industry job, it is unlikely you will find yourself designing a game. Most likely, you'll be responsible for writing code for specific parts of games. Or, if you are a digital artist, you might perform tasks like coloring and texturing 3-D models. As you gain experience and prove yourself, you will move on to positions of greater responsibility.

Work Is More Than Play

Working on a computer game can be fun, and there is often a lot of friendliness among team members. Keep in mind, however, that making a computer game is serious business to the company that is depending on it for income. As in any business, if you want to succeed, you need to conduct yourself professionally.

Responsibility is the key to success in any job. Being part of a company isn't like making your mods— you cannot work when and how you feel like it. Others depend on you to show up on time and get your work done on schedule.

Looking and behaving like a professional is a key to success in the digital development industry, just as in any other business.

Looking professional is important, too. How you are expected to dress will vary, depending on the type of company you work for. If you work for a large corporation such as Sony, you may be expected to dress in more traditional business attire such as slacks and a button-down shirt if you are male, or a pants suit or skirt and blouse if you are female. If you work for a small developer, more casual dress may be acceptable. In most cases, however, grungy T-shirts and frayed jeans are not acceptable attire, even in small companies. At any company, potential clients may drop by to discuss projects, and scruffy, unprofessional employees can create the impression of a badly run business.

Above all, do the best work you are capable of doing. This helps you, your coworkers, and the company you work for. Conducting yourself like a professional increases your chances of succeeding.

GLOSSARY

add-on Small program that provides additional features to an existing software program.

artificial intelligence Programming that allows a computer program to make decisions in response to user actions.

collaboration Working together with others on a project.

composition Arrangement of visual elements.

computer graphics Visual images created digitally on a computer.

copyright Right to reproduce audiovisual or printed material.

customizing Changing elements of an existing item to suit your personal taste.

digital Computer-based.

expansion Commercially produced add-on to an existing game.

forum Place on a Web site where people can exchange information.

graphics Visual images.

hacker Person who uses computers and computer code without permission.

instant messaging Technology that allows two people to "chat" via an e-mail–like method while they are both online.

Internet Worldwide network of computers.

intranet Private, Internet-like network of computers used within an organization.

portfolio Collection of samples of your work.

proprietary Owned by a particular person or company.

software development kit (SDK) Set of software tools for modding provided by a computer program's manufacturer.

source code Programming that makes up a computer application.

specs (specifications) Detailed instructions on how a product should be constructed and perform.

3-D modeling Using a computer program to produce three-dimensional images.

Web browser Software program that lets users interact with sites on the Internet.

Web page Screen on a Web site; most Web sites consist of a series of linked Web pages.

Web site Location on the Internet maintained by a person or organization.

FOR MORE INFORMATION

American Institute of Graphic Arts (AIGA)
164 Fifth Avenue
New York, NY 10010
(212) 807-1990
Web site: http://www.aiga.org
AIGA is a professional association for design.

Entertainment Software Association (ESA)
575 7th Street NW, Suite 300
Washington, DC 20004
Web site: http://www.theesa.com
The ESA is the U.S. association exclusively dedicated to
serving the business and public affairs needs of companies
that publish video and computer games for video game
consoles, personal computers, and the Internet.

Entertainment Software Association of Canada
130 Spadina Avenue, Suite 408
Toronto, ON M5V 2L4
Canada
(416) 620-7171
Web site: http://www.theesa.ca
ESA Canada is the Canadian counterpart to the ESA of
the United States (see above).

International Game Developers Association (IGDA)
19 Mantua Road
Mt. Royal, NJ 08061
(856) 423-2990

Web site: http://www.igda.org
The IGDA is committed to advancing the careers and enhancing the lives of game developers by connecting members with their peers, promoting professional development, and advocating on issues that affect the developer community.

Society of Graphic Designers of Canada—Student
  Career Info
Arts Court 2 Daly Avenue
Ottawa, ON K1N 6E2
Canada
Web site: http://www.gdc.net/for_students/careers.php
This Web site has information on Canadian colleges and universities with degrees in graphic design.

Software and Information Industry Association (SIIA)
1090 Vermont Avenue NW, Sixth Floor
Washington, DC 20005-4095
(202) 289-7442
Web site: http://www.siia.net
The SIIA is the principal trade association for the software and digital content industry.

Web Sites

Due to the changing nature of Internet links, the Rosen Publishing Group, Inc., has developed an online list of Web sites related to the subject of this book. This site is updated regularly. Please use this link to access the list:

http://www.rosenlinks.com/dcb/skmo

FOR FURTHER READING

Facts On File. *Ferguson's Careers in Focus: Computer and Video Game Design*. New York, NY: Facts On File, 2006.

Grebler, Eric B. *3D Game Programming for Teens*. Boston, MA: Course Technology/Thomson Learning, 2006.

Harbour, James S. *Visual Basic Game Programming for Teens*. Boston, MA: Course Technology/Thomson Learning, 2004.

Murdock, Kelly L. *3D Game Animation for Dummies*. Indianapolis, IN: For Dummies, 2005.

Pardew, Les. *Game Art for Teens*. Boston, MA: Course Technology/Thomson Learning, 2004.

Pardew, Les. *Game Design for Teens*. Boston, MA: Course Technology/Thomson Learning, 2004.

Sethi, Maneesh. *Game Design for Teens*, 2nd ed. Boston, MA: Course Technology/Thomson Learning, 2005.

Sethi, Maneesh. *Web Design for Teens*. Boston, MA: Course Technology/Thomson Learning, 2004.

BIBLIOGRAPHY

Camargo, Caio. "Modding: Changing the Game, Changing the Industry." *The ACM Student*. Retrieved April 23, 2007 (http://www.acm.org/crossroads/xrds13-2/modding.html).

Duffy, Jill. "6th Annual Salary Survey." *Game Developer*, April 2007.

Edge Online. "Get Into Games." Retrieved April 23, 2007 (http://www.edge-online.co.uk/archives/2005/07/get_intogames_1.php).

Education Online. "Careers for Game Design." Retrieved May 12, 2007 (http://www.educationcenteronline.org/articles/Design-Schools/Careers-for-Games-Design.html).

Evans, Meryl. "Careers in Web Design." Informit.com. Retrieved May 12, 2007 (http://www.informit.com/guides/content.asp?g = webdesign&seqNum = 175&rl = 1).

Hyman, Paul. "Video Game Companies Encourage 'Modders.'" *The Hollywood Reporter*. April 9, 2004. Retrieved May 5, 2007 (http://www.hollywoodreporter.com/hr/search/article_display.jsp?vnu_content_id = 1000484956).

Information Architecture Institute. "Salary Survey, 2006." 2007. Retrieved May 30, 2007 (http://iainstitute.org/pg/salary_survey_2006.php).

International Game Developers Association. "Breaking In: Preparing for Your Career in Games." Retrieved April 23, 2007 (http://www.igda.org/breakingin).

Kushner, David. "It's a Mod, Mod World." IEEE Spectrum Careers Online. Retrieved April 23, 2007 (http://www.spectrum.ieee.org/careers/careerstemplate.jsp?ArticleId=i020203).

Kushner, David. "The Mod Squad." *Popular Science*. 2006. Retrieved May 5, 2007 (http://www.popsci.com/popsci/computerselec/0678d4d03cb84010vgnvcm1000004eecbccdrcrd.html).

OEDb Online Education Database. "The Ultimate Guide to Video Game Degrees and Careers." Retrieved April 23, 2007 (http://oedb.org/library/features/video-game-degrees-and careers).

INDEX

About the Author

Jeri Freedman has a B.A. from Harvard University. She is the author of eighteen young-adult nonfiction books, many of which have been published by Rosen Publishing. Under the name Ellen Foxxe, she is the coauthor of two alternate history science fiction novels. Freedman lives in Boston.

Photo Credits

Cover and title page (montage clockwise from top left) © www.istockphoto.com/Antonis Papantoniou; © www.istockphoto.com/Abel Leão; © www.istockphoto.com/Alexandru Vulpe; © www.istockphoto.com/Andrzej Burak; © www.istockphoto.com/Lisa Thornberg; © www.istockphoto.com/Linda Bucklin; p. 4 (mod) Fallout: Between Good & Evil. Image by Mad_Eye. (www.towerofcreation.com); pp. 8, 11, 22, 24, 38 (top), 46 © AP Images; p. 13 © Jim Doberman/Getty Images; p. 15 © Patrik Giardino/Corbis; pp. 18, 20 (bottom), 23 Shutterstock.com; p. 20 (top) © Darryl Bush/San Francisco Chronicle/Corbis; pp. 28, 44 © Getty Images; p. 32 © AFP/Getty Images; p. 36 © Michael Smith/Getty Images; p. 48 © Pat LaCroix/Getty Images; p. 50 © www.istockphoto.com/Gustaf Brundin; p. 50 (computer screen inset) © www.istockphoto.com/Antonis Papantoniou; p. 54 © Marcus Mok/Asia Images Group/ age fotostock.

Designer: Nelson Sá; **Editor:** Christopher Roberts